KT-224-688

700039821335

www.raintreepublishers.co.uk
Visit our website to find out
more information about
Raintree books.

To order:
☎ Phone 0845 6044371
🖹 Fax +44 (0) 1865 312263
🖳 Email myorders@raintreepublishers.co.uk

Customers from outside the UK please telephone +44 1865 312262

Raintree is an imprint of Capstone Global Library Limited,
a company incorporated in England and Wales having its
registered office at 7 Pilgrim Street, London, EC4V 6LB
– Registered company number: 6695582

Text © Capstone Global Library Limited 2013
First published in hardback in 2013
The moral rights of the proprietor have been asserted.

All rights reserved. No part of this publication may be reproduced in
any form or by any means (including photocopying or storing it in any
medium by electronic means and whether or not transiently or incidentally
to some other use of this publication) without the written permission of
the copyright owner, except in accordance with the provisions of the
Copyright, Designs and Patents Act 1988 or under the terms of a licence
issued by the Copyright Licensing Agency, Saffron House, 6–10 Kirby
Street, London EC1N 8TS (www.cla.co.uk). Applications for the copyright
owner's written permission should be addressed to the publisher.

Edited by Daniel Nunn, Rebecca Rissman, and Sian Smith
Designed by Cynthia Della-Rovere
Picture research by Mica Brancic
Production by Victoria Fitzgerald
Originated by Capstone Global Library Ltd
Printed and bound in China by South China Printing
 Company Ltd

ISBN 978 1 406 23904 1
16 15 14 13 12
10 9 8 7 6 5 4 3 2 1

British Library Cataloguing in Publication Data
Nunn, Daniel.
Numbers in French. -- (World languages. Numbers)
448.2'421-dc23
A full catalogue record for this book is available from the British Library.

Acknowledgements
We would like to thank Shutterstock for permission to reproduce
photographs: © Agorohov, © Aleksandrs Poliscuks, © Alex James Bramwell,
© Andreas Gradin, © Andrey Armyagov, © archidea, © Arogant, © atoss,
© Baloncici, © Benjamin Mercer, © blackpixel, © charles taylor, © Chris
Bradshaw, © cloki, © dcwcreations, © DenisNata, © Diana Taliun, © Eric
Isselée, © Erik Lam, © Fatseyeva, © Feng Yu, © g215, © Hywit Dimyadi, ©
Iv Nikolny, © J. Waldron, © jgl247, © joingate, © karam Miri, © Karkas, ©
kedrov, © LittleMiss, © Ljupco Smokovski, © Lori Sparkia, © Max Krasnov,
© Michelangelus, © Mike Flippo, © mimo, © Nordling, © Olga Popova,
© Pavel Sazonov, © pics fine, © Rosery, © Ruth Black, © Shmel, © Stacy
Barnett, © Steve Collender, © Suzanna, © Tania Zbrodko, © topseller, ©
Vasina Natalia, © Veniamin Kraskov, © Vinicius Tupinamba, © Volodymyr
Krasyuk, © Vorm in Beeld, © Winston Link, © xpixel.

Cover photographs reproduced with permission of Shutterstock: number 1
(© Leigh Prather), number 2 (© Glovatskiy), number 3 (© Phuriphat).
Back cover photographs of toys of reproduced with permission of
Shutterstock (© joingate, © Lori Sparkia, © Michelangelus, © Agorohov, ©
Tania Zbrodko).

We would like to thank Séverine Ribierre for her invaluable assistance in the
preparation of this book.

Every effort has been made to contact copyright holders of material
reproduced in this book. Any omissions will be rectified in subsequent
printings if notice is given to the publisher.

Contents

Un

un chien

Il y a un chien.

There is one dog.

un pull

Il y a un pull.

There is one jumper.

3

Deux

un chat

Il y a deux chats.

There are two cats.

une chaussure

Il y a deux chaussures.

There are two shoes.

Trois

une fille

Il y a trois filles.

There are three girls.

une chaise

Il y a trois chaises.

There are three chairs.

Quatre

un oiseau

Il y a quatre oiseaux.

There are four birds.

un coussin

Il y a quatre coussins.

There are four cushions.

Cinq

un jouet

Il y a cinq jouets.

There are five toys.

un livre

Il y a cinq livres.

There are five books.

Six

un manteau

Il y a six manteaux.

There are six coats.

un crayon

Il y a six crayons.

There are six pencils.

Sept

une orange

Il y a sept oranges.

There are seven oranges.

un biscuit

Il y a sept biscuits.

There are seven biscuits.

Huit

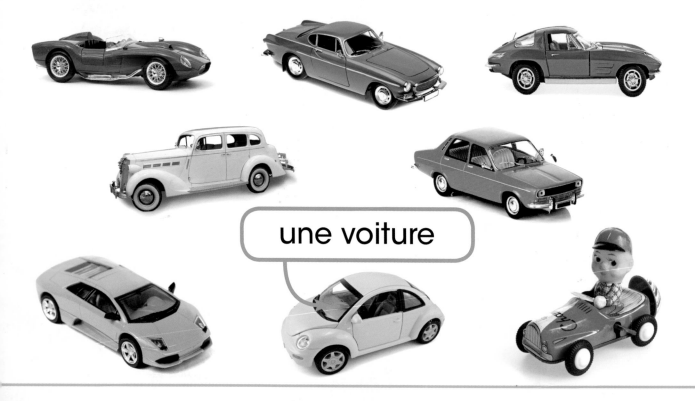

une voiture

Il y a huit voitures.

There are eight cars.

un chapeau

Il y a huit chapeaux.

There are eight hats.

Neuf

un ballon

Il y a neuf ballons.

There are nine balloons.

une bougie

Il y a neuf bougies.

There are nine candles.

Dix

une pomme

Il y a dix pommes.

There are ten apples.

une fleur

Il y a dix fleurs.

There are ten flowers.

Dictionary

French word	How to say it	English word
ballon / ballons	bal-lon	balloon / balloons
biscuit / biscuits	bis-kwee	biscuit / biscuits
bougie / bougies	boo-gee	candle / candles
chaise / chaises	shez	chair / chairs
chapeau / chapeaux	sha-po	hat / hats
chat / chats	sha	cat / cats
chaussure / chaussures	sho-sur	shoe / shoes
chien	she-an	dog
cinq	sank	five
coussin / coussins	coo-san	cushion / cushions
crayon / crayons	kray-on	pencil / pencils
deux	duh	two
dix	deece	ten
fille / filles	feey	girl / girls
fleur / fleurs	flur	flower / flowers
huit	weet	eight

French word	How to say it	English word
il y a	eel-ee-a	there is / there are
jouet / jouets	joo-ay	toy / toys
livre / livres	leevre	book / books
manteau / manteaux	man-toe	coat / coats
neuf	nuf	nine
oiseau / oiseaux	wa-zo	bird / birds
orange / oranges	or-onj	orange / oranges
pomme / pommes	pom	apple / apples
pull	pull	jumper
quatre	katre	four
sept	set	seven
six	seece	six
trois	trwa	three
un / une	un / oo-n	a
un / une	un / oo-n	one
voiture / voitures	vwa-ture	car / cars

Index

Notes for parents and teachers
In French, nouns are either masculine or feminine. The word for "a" or "one" changes accordingly – either un (masculine) or une (feminine).